LET'S CELEBRATE 365

Somewhere in the world on any given day of the year, there is a festival or ceremony taking place - either sacred, secular or spiritual. Although each of these is visually very different, the linking commonality for them all is that they provide an annual opportunity for the participants to demonstrate and express their indigenous beliefs, customs and heritage. These extraordinary rituals and celebrations often take place against a backdrop of some of the world's most stunning landscapes. The festivals are always spectacular; the fantastic imagery is created by the participants themselves - not by Disney or Hollywood.

In the early part of 1975 Britain was in chaos, and industry had ceased to function due to the Miners coming out on strike. The country was on a three-day week and most businesses were making massive redundancies. I had been a 'creative' in advertising for the previous ten years, producing television commercials for many of Britain's leading Brands - and was also made redundant. There appeared to be few creative opportunities left for me at that time in th
and I was therefore very fortunate to see in a broadsheet newspaper a position advertise
NIRTV (the national TV station of Iran) for a TV Reporter/Producer to be based in Tehra
I was an advertising creative; I had never reported for television in my life. But I got the jo
a month later arrived in Tehran where I was to replace the incumbent Reporter/Produce
English, who had just returned from Vietnam where he had been covering the Fall of S
and had decided whilst there that his ambition to become a Television Darts Commer
rather than a Foreign Correspondent would provide a more secure, and certainly, safer c

So after two weeks, I was given my first assignment. "Prepare yourself to go to the North Pole - tonight - and then when you've been there, you can go to the South Pole".

"Why?" I asked. "We will be the first Iranian TV team to go there" I was told.

A couple of hours later, after I had worked out how we might possibly get from Tehran to the North Pole that evening, my boss, the Iranian Executive Producer, told me that he'd changed his mind and that I could go to the North Pole the following week. I was to go immediately to Australia "to get Malcolm Fraser, the Prime Minister". So I informed my Iranian crew about this decision, which made them a lot happier, and we got our gear together for the southern hemisphere. However, a further two hours later I was handed the air tickets for this trip. But they were to Delhi, not Melbourne or Canberra. "You'll go to Delhi tonight - make sure you get the Prime Minister Indira Gandhi, or I'll fine you," the Exec. Prod ordered me.

So off I went to India to interview the most powerful woman in the world. It was a terrifying experience for an ex-ad. creative. But somehow I got through it, and life then became a roller-coaster of weekly trips around the world interviewing world leaders and dodging bullets in an increasing number of dangerous war zones.

The Shah (who I ultimately worked for) believed that a coup was imminent and that the country would be overrun from the north (Soviet Union) by the Communists. So a number of reportages that I carried out were related to the rise in influence of Communist groups, particularly in Europe.

It was impractical to make a thirty minute programme simply by stringing together endless interviews of 'talking-heads' so I began to look for interesting visual imagery that I could use as a 'peg' to hang these discussions on. It happened, mostly by luck, that I found festivals and ceremonies taking place in the filmic vicinity of my reportages so as I journeyed around the world, I began specifically to look for these. I not only filmed them for my weekly television programme, but I also began to shoot many photographs for my own archives. As my library began to expand, I became more passionate (and knowledgeable) about the subject.

LET'S CELEBRATE 365 therefore is the result of twenty-six years of amazing journeys around the globe. It's taken a great deal of time as so many of the festivals happen concurrently due to the religious date, the new year, the phases of the moon and other annual patterns within the calendar. The festivals that appear in this book are representative, mostly, of global festival activity in the Buddhist, Christian, Hindu, Islamic, Jain, Jewish, and Pagan worlds but there are thousands more that I still have been unable to witness yet. Some countries have festivals almost daily. I have a calendar of festivals in Bali numbering around two hundred - a month. Every weekend during the summer months is *fiesta* time in Spain and Portugal, and India is said to have more festivals than days in the year.

But **LET'S CELEBRATE 365** also has an important historic and archival value, for acculturation is rapid and it is probable that some of the images here will never be repeated due to changes in life-styles of the ethnic groups involved. Global technological advances will surely impact on indigeneous populations and inevitably cause change.

FESTIVAL:
Maha Kumbh Mela

Country, Place and Location:
Prayag, near Allahabad, Uttar Pradesh, India

Religion:
Hindu. One of the world's oldest living religions which predates recorded history. Over 800 million adherents worldwide

Date of Celebration:
January. This festival is celebrated once every 12 years and has been taking place for around 3000 years

Prayag - a Hindi word for 'confluence' - is where the waters of India's three sacred rivers, the Ganges, Yamuna and mythical Saraswati meet. It is the holiest place in Hinduism. In 2001, up to 70 million pilgrims are estimated to have attended the forty-two days of religious pilgrimage intertwined with carnival that is the Maha Kumbh Mela, the great Festival of Elixir celebrating the triumphant recovery of the Nectar of Immortality.

Naked Nagas of the Nirvani Akhara (religious army) dash headlong into the icy waters of the Ganges at dawn on the auspicious day of Makar Sankranti. There is fierce competition between these religious armies to be the first into the waters. The Nagas (warrior-monks) take the ascetic life to the extreme - renouncing all worldly pleasures and pursuits. They consider their ash coating to be the only clothing they require, for they say that punishing the body is the path to Enlightenment.

FESTIVAL:
Maha Kumbh Mela

Country, Place and Location:
Prayag, near Allahabad, Uttar Pradesh, India

Religion:
Hindu. One of the world's oldest living religions which predates recorded history. Over 800 million adherents worldwide

Date of Celebration:
January. This festival is celebrated once every 12 years and has been taking place for around 3000 years

The aim of Sadhus (holy men) is to reach Enlightenment in this life rather than the next; to do this many practise extreme austerities. Amar Bharati is an *Ek-Bahu* Baba who has kept his arm above his head for nearly 20 years; the straighter the arm and closer to the head the better. This is quite a handicap as everything then has to be done with the left hand - the 'dirty' hand.

FESTIVAL:
Maha Kumbh Mela

Country, Place and Location:
Prayag, near Allahabad, Uttar Pradesh, India

Religion:
Hindu. One of the world's oldest living religions which predates recorded history. There are over 800 million adherents worldwide

Date of Celebration:
January. This festival is celebrated once every 12 years and has been taking place for around 3000 years

1: Just after dawn on the day of Makar Sankranti, the day on which, according to the priests, the planets aligned in a formation not seen for 144 years, the dreadlocked Nagas of the Nirvani Akhara (religious army) await to enter the sacred icy waters of the Ganges. Their ghostly appearance is achieved by coating their bodies with the ashes of the dead.

2: These are members of the naked dreadlocked Nagas, feared for their magical powers. The warrior-monks take their ascetic life to extremes, renouncing all worldly pleasures and pursuits. The ash from the dead with which they coat their bodies is the only covering they require.

3: Young boys, attired in the most opulent and lavish of ceremonial costumes, take on a temporary gender change during the Kumbh and are worshipped as living female Goddesses. Their feet are not allowed to touch the ground and they are carried everywhere by their fathers or guardians.

FESTIVAL:
La Sartiglia

Country, Place and Location:
Oristano, Sardinia, Italy

Religion:
Catholic. Over 1 billion adherents worldwide

Date of Celebration:
February

La Sartiglia was created around 1543 by Canon Giovanni Dessi. The term *Sartiglia* is derived from the Spanish *Sortija* which comes from the Latin word *sorticula* (=ring) and *sors* (=fortune) and it is 'fortune' that is the predominant element of the festival.

In Oristano, Paganism and Catholicism have developed side by side. Each year, the finest horseman of the region is elected *Cumponidori*. For one day, he is no longer a man; he becomes a masked God-Horseman. His horse is his throne and his word is absolute. His equestrian skills are put to the ultimate of tests and if, during the course of the day, the God-Horseman falls from his horse, then the fortune of the entire region for the coming twelve months will be in jeopardy.

After the completion of the dressing ceremony and accompanied by his horsemen, the *Cumponidori* goes towards his equestrian fate. The crowd is waiting for him, prays for him, applauses, encourages him while he blesses them *(sa remada)* with a sceptre made of violets.

FESTIVAL:
Mardi Gras

Country, Place and Location:
French Guiana, Cayenne

Religion:
Catholic

Date of Celebration:
February: Fat Tuesday - traditionally the last day before the fasting of Lent begins

In centuries past during Lent, foods such as meat, butter and eggs would be forbidden so stocks had to be eaten up by the day before, a wonderful excuse for a huge feast on Mardi Gras - Fat Tuesday.

The celebrations are usually frenetic, and despite the festival's religious origins, the enduring image of Mardi Gras is of outrageous costumes and dancing and naked flesh.

FESTIVAL:
Grand Summons of the Labuleng Monastery

Country, Place and Location:
Labrang, Autonomous Region of East Tibet. Labrang is also known as Xiahe

Religion:
Buddhist. Founded 2500 years ago in India. Over 300 million adherents worldwide

Date of Celebration:
First lunar month of Tibetan calendar, heralding the start of the Tibetan New Year (Feb.)

Established in 1709, in the 48th year of the Kangxi reign of the Qing dynasty, the Labuleng Monastery is considered to be the leading Tibetan monastery town outside Lhasa and is the centre for the Yellow Hat sect of Tibetan Buddhism. Before communism came to Tibet, China and Mongolia, there were approximately 1 million Buddhist monks. During the Cultural Revolution at the height of persecution, this dropped to less than 21,000.

1: During the festival, the entire monkhood attend the great debate in the presence of the Living Buddha, praying for the Enlightened One's blessings. The altitude here is 10,700 ft and the temperature on this day was -27.

2: The high-point of the four-day festival is the series of Cham dances, signifying Good versus Evil, performed by masked monks. It is very rare to see the dancer-monks unmasked; these two were waiting in one of the little courtyards behind the monastery.

3. Each element of the dances is heralded by fanfares played on 8ft long trombones, here being carried down by the monks to the main courtyard of the temple.

FESTIVAL:
Grand Summons of the Labuleng Monastery

Country, Place and Location:
Labrang, Autonomous Region of East Tibet. Labrang is also known as Xiahe

Religion:
Buddhist. founded 2500 years ago in India. Over 300 million adherents worldwide

Date of Celebration:
First lunar month of Tibetan calendar, heralding the start of the Tibetan New Year; usually early February

1: Monks await the arrival of the Living Buddha.

2: Before the Great Debate in the presence of the Living Buddha, a majestic procession of the senior monkhood takes place.

As a nation, despite our cultural and religious diversity, we are not very good at understanding the ways of "others". I hope therefore that **LET'S CELEBRATE 365** can offer an insight into the major religious faiths and beliefs through their annual festivals, ceremonies and pilgrimages, Many of these rituals and celebrations that have been carefully choreographed through the centuries are, in my view, truly cultural wonders of the world. For the celebrants, believing in gods and the spirits is like an insurance policy. They participate in these festivals because, for the majority, their wish is to live another life - in a different and more fortunate form.

Although they do not appear on the orthodox travel map, these celebrations are readily accessible to the adventurous traveller. But the pace of change is startling and 21st century acculturation is bound to have an impact on these virtual "snapshots in time" which continue to offer a rare opportunity to discover a place and its culture.

JANUARY HIGHLIGHTS:
Bolivia: Alasitas "buy from me" Fair, La Paz; Festival of Abundance,La Paz
Brazil: Celebration to the Goddess of the Sea, Copacabana Beach, Rio de Janeiro; Festival of Sao Sebastiao
Burma: Celebration of Independence Day, Royal Lake, Rangoon (Yangon)
Colombia: Carnaval de Blancas y Negros, Pasto; Carnaval del Diablo, Riosucio
Domenica: Our Lady of La Altagracia
England: Wassailing the Apple Trees, Carhampton, Somerset (17th); Plough Monday (1st Monday after Epiphany)
India: Pongal, Tamil Nadu and Ahmedabad; Kalachakra Tantra, Sarnath nr. Banares
Italy: Feast of the Gift, Castiglione di Garfagnana, Lucca; Night of the Biso, Faenza, Ravenna
Jamaica: Epiphany
Japan: Ganjitsu, Meiji-jingu, Tokyo
Malaysia: Thaipusam, Batu Caves
Mexico: Day of the Kings
Philippines: Ati-Atihan, Kalibo, Panay; Black Nazarene Procession, Quiapo Church, Manila
Poland: Crossing of the River Jordan, Sanok
Russia: Russian Orthodox Christmas Eve and Day
Spain: Santa Cruz de Tenerife, Cadiz
Sri Lanka: Duruthu Poya perahera, Kelaniya, Colombo
Turkey: Devi Guresi (Camel-Fighting), Kusadasi

FESTIVAL:
Mahamastakabhisheka

Country, Place and Location:
Shravana Belagola ("the monk on top of the hill") near Hassan, Karnataka, India

Religion:
Jainism. One of the oldest living religions. It has no beginning and predates recorded history. There are about 6 million adherents, mostly in India

Date of Celebration:
Usually every twelve years

MAHA means Great, MASTA Head ABHISHEK Washing - The Great Head Washing Festival - has been taking place since March 13, 981 A.D when the gigantic monolithic statue of Bahubali was commissioned; 59 feet high and carved from one piece of granite, the statue is probably the largest of its kind in the world. Carved between 978 - 993 A.D the statue stands at the top of Indragiri Hill 3347 ft above sea-level in Southern India, at a site now considerd by World Heritage to be one of the New Seven Wonders of the World.

Bahubali, or Sri Gomatheswar, was the 98th, and favourite son, of the legendary Adinatha - the first *Tirthankara* - the mythical, enlightened sages of Jainism who have achieved *Siddha* Total Knowledge. The 24th and last *Tirthankara* to achieve *Siddha* was Lord Mahavir about 2,500 years ago.

1: During the climax of the festival, priests and devotees standing on top of the specially-erected scaffolding chant holy mantras and ritually pour tens of thousands of litres of milk, honey, jewellery, flowers and precious herbs and spices over the head of the statue. Whilst flowing down the body of Bahubali the sacred offerings are believed to acquire a powerful charge of spiritual energy. Collected at the feet of the statue and distibuted in glass bottles the magical liquids are considered to assist devotees in their quest for enlightenment.

2: Milk, the fourth liquid in the Sequence of 21 *Abhiskekas*, is poured from *kalashas* on to the head of Bahubali.

3: The ceremony is supervised by monks of the extreme, and naked, Digambara ("Sky-Clad") sect who have renounced all clothing and worldly goods.

4. At the same time as the colossus of Bahubali is being washed, another washing ceremony is taking place in the town at the ancient temple of Bhandara Basadi. *Sarvathobhadhra Puja* is a special kind of *puja* where images of all 24 *Tirthankaras* are worshipped simultaneously.

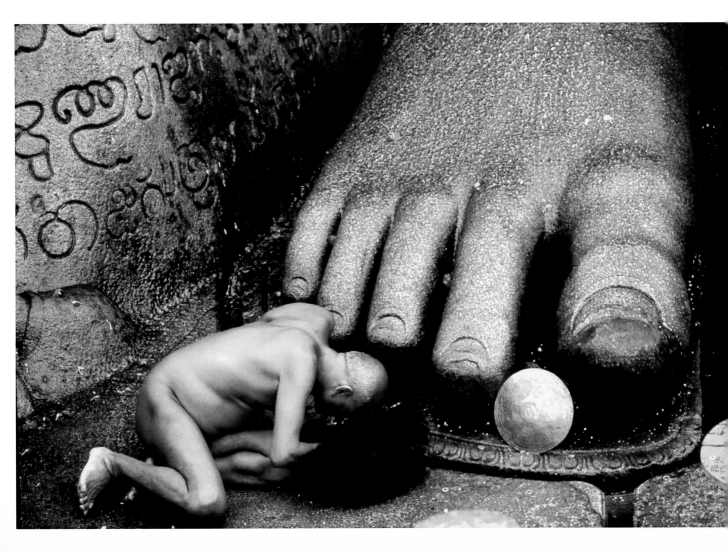

CEREMONY:
Diksha

Country, Place and Location:
Shravana Belagola, near Hassan, Karnataka, India

Religion:
Jainism. One of the oldest living religions. It has no beginning and predates recorded history. There are about 6 million adherents, mostly in India

Date of Ceremony:
Infrequently. It is extremely rare to witness *Diksha* but I was able to attend this ceremony during the auspicious Festival of Mahamastakabhisheka (QV)

During the Festival, thirty-six men and women underwent the initiation of becoming Jain Monks *(Muni)* or Nuns, by discarding for ever all their worldly possessions, and in the case of the *Muni*, all their clothes. The ascetic *Muni* of the naked Digambara ("sky-clad") sect may only possess books, a *Picchi* (a peacock-feather broom to sweep the ground) and a *Kamandalu* (a tin pot for water). They may beg for food and water, but just once a day.

Monks and Nuns must abandon all forms of attachment to their self and body and they must cultivate an indifferent attitude towards pain and pleasure, comfort and discomfort,. To join their Sect they must undergo the most extreme, and painful, element of their initiation - the practice of *keshlunch* in which their entire hair is pulled out by the roots, leaving their head totally bald.

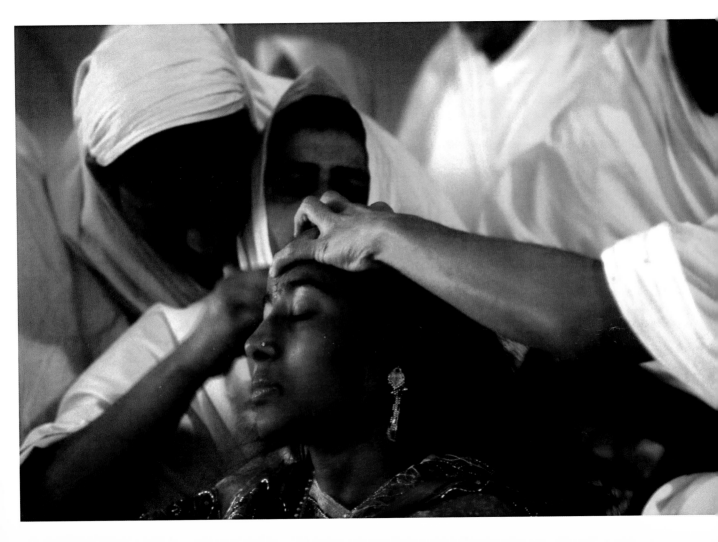

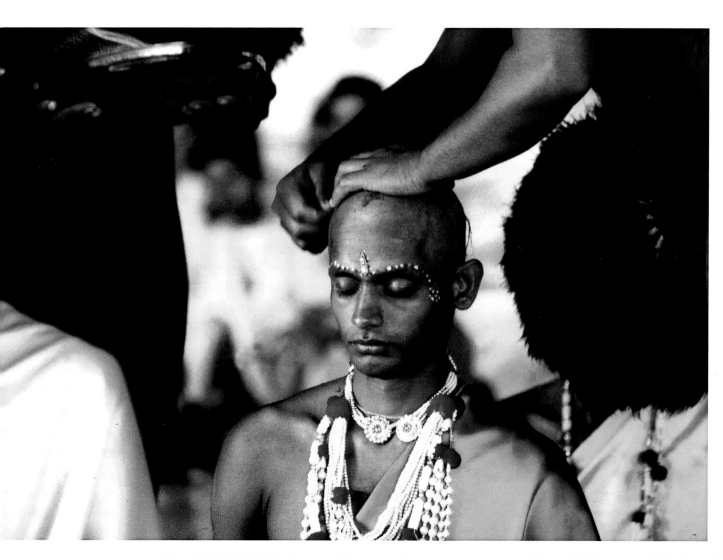

FESTIVAL:
Purim

Country, Place and Location:
Stamford Hill, North London, England

Religion:
Judaism. There are about 14 million adherents worldwide

Date of Celebration:
March/April

In the Old Testament, Esther is the wife of the Persian King Ahaseurus. She is considered a heroine of the Jewish people for she engineered the overturning of a decree that allowed the people to annihilate the Jews.

According to the *Talmud*, the name Esther is derived from the Hebrew word *nistar* meaning 'to be hidden', and so during the carnival atmosphere of Purim the children, in particular, hide behind elaborate masks. It is also a time for giving and everyone is required to give at least two gifts, usually of food and drink; anyone who puts out their hand should also receive something.

The wearer of this extraordinary mask is a Hasidic boy of 10.

FESTIVAL:
500th Anniversary of Guru Anghad Devi Ji

Country, Place and Location:
Khadoor Sahib, Northern Punjab, India

Religion:
Sikh. Founded 500 years ago in Punjab by Guru Nanak (1469 - 1539). There are 19 million adherents worldwide

Date of Celebration:
April

The founder of the Sikh movement, Guru Nanak, sought to reconcile both Hindu and Muslim faiths by taking a middle path that embraced both of the other two. Sikhism is derived from the word *sikka* meaning disciple.

Khadoor Sahib is a small, but important, village close to the border with Pakistan which over the centuries was visited by each of the eight Great Masters (Sikh gurus). In 2004 an estimated 5 million pilgrims attended the festival.

Sikhs adopt the name *singh* which means lion and signifies courage, and they are readily identifiable by their turbans. They take a vow not to cut their hair and beard (signifying renunciation) and to abstain from alcohol and cigarettes. The ideal Sikh-Man is a Warrior Saint; his sword signifies bravery and he must be prepared to fight and sacrifice his life in defense of his faith. The iron bracelet on his wrist signifies morality. As one Sikh told me "No Crown, No King, No Hair, No Sikh!"

FESTIVAL:
Aboakyer, or Deer Hunting, Festival

Country, Place and Location:
Winneba, Central Region, Ghana

Religion:
African Traditional, honouring the fetish War God Apa Sekum

Date of Celebration:
May 1

The close relationship between hunting and the sacred is found throughout traditional religious rituals and festivals the world over. It is the importance of food and security which comes from food that is at the heart of this festival.

The Aboakyer Festival is celebrated by the Efutu in honour of their tribal god *Penkye Otu*. The Efutu believe that the land that they occupied about three hundred years ago in the Central Region of Ghana only came to them as a result of their worshipping *Penkye Otu*. This tribal god still helps and protects them, and therefore as an expression of gratitude, the God receives every May an annual sacrifice of a deer from the people.

The festival is celebrated by two *Asafo* (ancient warrior) companies - Number One: *Tuafo* and Number Two: *Dentsifo*. The Efutu believe that if Number One Company wins the hunt contest, there will be peace and prosperity in the coming year but if Number Two wins, it will be a year of famine and war.

These are members of Number One Company: *Tuafo* after their successful hunt. So peace and prosperity will therefore reign with the Efutu for another year.

FESTIVAL:
Maulidi

Country, place and location:
Lamu Island, Kenya

Religion:
Islam. Founded by the Prophet Mohammed about 1,400 years ago in Arabia. Islam is the world's fastest growing religion; there are about 950 million adherents worlwide

Date of Celebration:
May/June

The island's Swahili capital was at the peak of its civilization from the 17th to the 19th century but faded in power and wealth as the slave trade died. Lamu has survived centuries of conquest and today its culture is a mix of African, Arab, Asian, Indian, and Portuguese. *Maulidi* presents an opportunity for the women of this Islamic region to demonstrate, within a predominately matriachal society, their sense of identity and personality on an island where home ownership is dominated by women.

FESTIVAL:
Maulidi

Country, place and location:
Lamu Island, Kenya

Religion:
Islam. Founded by the Prophet Mohammed about 1,400 years ago in Arabia. Islam is the world's fastest growing religion; there are about 950 million adherents worlwide

Date of Celebration:
May/June

The annual *Maulidi* which celebrates the Prophet Mohammed's birth draws pilgrims from all over East Africa and the Indian Ocean to the World Heritage-protected island site of Lamu, close to Zanzibar. Body painting, particularly of the hands and feet, forms an important element for the women who attend.

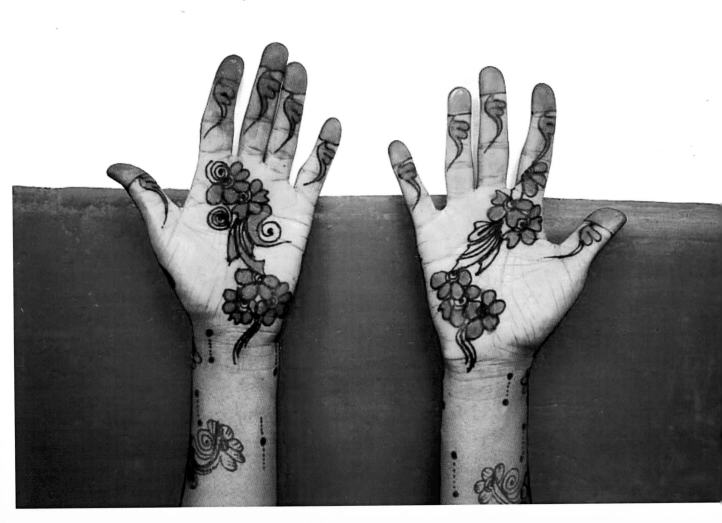

FEBRUARY HIGHLIGHTS:

Bangladesh: Saraswati Puja
Bolivia: Virgin of Canelaria, Aiqile; Carnival, Oruro
Brazil: Mardi Gras, Rio de Janeiro
Bulgaria: Vine-Growers Day, Trifon Zarezan
Cambodia: Tet
Caribbean: Mardi Gras
China: Chinese New Year; Fuxi Temple Celebrations; Spring Festival; Temple Fair, Baiyunguan
Colombia: Carnaval, Barranquilla
Cyprus: Apokreo (50 days before Orthodox Easter)
England: Shrove Tuesday/Pancake Day, Olney, Bucks
France: Carnival des Pecheurs, Dunkirk
Greece: Carnival, Patras, Thebes
Hong Kong: Lantern Festival
India: Jaisalmer Desert Festival; Saraswati Puja; Mahashivratri
Italy: Carnival Week, particularly Venice; also Ivrea, nr. Turin; Valtorta; Ronciglione
Japan: Setsuban Bean-Scattering
Laos: Magha Puja (Makka Bu-Saa)
Malta: Carnival
Singapore: Chinese New
Slovenia: Kurentovanje, Ptuj
Spain: Fiesta de Santa Agueda, Segovia
Switzerland: Lucerne Festival; Fasnacht, Basel
Thailand: Chao Mae Lim Ko Nieo Fair
Tibet: Tibetan New Year; Great Prayer Festival
U.S.A: Mardi Gras, New Orleans
Vietnam: Tet Nguyen Dan

MARCH HIGHLIGHTS:

Bangladesh: Holi Festival
Bolivia: Semana Santa 158km walk - Copocabana to La Paz
China: Flower Fair, Chengdu
Colombia: Semana Santa, Popoyan and Mompos
Egypt: Coptic "Sniffing the Breeze", Sharm-el-Nessum
Guatemala: Pilgrimage to Christ of Golgotha, Chajul; Semana Santa, Antigua Guatemala
Hawaii: Oahu Kite Festival; Prince Kuhio Festival
India: Ganguar Festival, Udaipur
Indonesia: Garebeg Besar Ceremony, Idul Adha, Yogyakarta
Italy: Good Friday, Scala Santa, Rome; Holy Week, Taranto; Easter Sunday, Scorppio del Carto
Norway: Karasjok Easter Festival
Peru: Semana Santa, Cuzco and Ayacucho
Philippines: Holy Week: Crucifixion Re-Enactment, San Fernando (San Pedro Cutud); Moriones Festival, Marinduque Island
Poland: The Procession of One Hundred Horses
Sardinia: Holy Week, Cagliari
Spain: Semana Santa, Seville; also Carmona, Cartagena, Cuenca, Lorca, Malaga

APRIL HIGHLIGHTS:

Bolivia: Fiesta de la Papa (Potato Festival), Betanzos
Burma: Thingyan Water Festival
China: Qing Ming Festival (Festival of Pure Brightness)
Hong Kong: Festival of the Heavenly Queen, Goddess of Fishermen
Japan: Cherry Blossom Festival, Festival of the Shrine, Toyama-Ken; Sanno Matsuri, Hida district, Takayama
Korea: Yeongdeung Festival, Jindo
Laos: Pi Mai Festival
Poland: Cracow, The Sufferings of the Archbrotherhood
Sri Lanka: Tamil New Year
Thailand: Songkran
Tunisia: Sparrow Hawk Festival, El Haouaria, nr. Nabeul
Vietnam: Thankh Minh - Holiday of the Dead

MAY HIGHLIGHTS:

Argentina: Lujan pilgrimage
Belgium: 1000 year old Kattenwoensdog Cat Festival, Ypres
Bolivia: Fiesta de la Cruz, Tarija
Burma: The Thrice-Blessed Day on the Full Moon, Shwedagon Paya, Yangon
Cambodia: Chrat Prea Angkai (ceremonial beginning to sowing season)
China: Miaio Peoples Festival, Guizhou, Hunan, Hubei, Sichuan Provinces; Paomao Fair, Kangding, Sichuan
Czech Republic: Folk Festival, Vicnov
England: Pilgrimage to the Shrine of Our Lady at Walsingham, Norfolk; Obby Oss, Padstow, Cornwall (May Day); Cornish Furry Dance, Helston (8th)
France: Gypsy Festival, Les-Santes-Maries-de-la-Mer, Camargue; Seaman's Festival, Honfleur, Normandy
Greece: Anastenaria - Fire-Walking Festival, Agia Eleni; also Langada, nr. Thessalonika
Hong Kong: Cheung Chan Bun Festival
India: Trichur Elephant Pooram, Thiruvambadi, Kerala
Italy: Festa di San Domenico e i Serpari, Festival of Snakes, Cocullo; Giostra della Quintana, Foligno (Joust)
Japan: Tosho-gu Grand Festival, Nikko-shi, nr. Tokyo (18th)
Korea: Chunhyang Festival, Namwon
Laos: Visakha Puja - Birth, Enlightenment and Death of Buddha
Peru: Andinism week, Huaraz; Qoyllur Rit'i - Pilgrimage to Quispicanchis, Cuzco district
Sardinia: Sagra di Sant' Efisio, Cagliari
Thailand: Visakha Puja Day; Yasothon Bun Bangfai Rocket Festival, Phaya Thaen Park
Vietnam: Birth of Buddha celebration

FESTIVAL:
Festival of the Goddess Amman

Country, Place and Location:
Temple of Sri Mahamariamman, Kuala Lumpur, Malaysia

Religion:
Hindu. One of the world's oldest living religion which predates recorded history. Over 800 million adherents worldwide

Date of Celebration:
July

For the Tamil women of Kuala Lumpur the Goddess Amman is their special protector and benefactor. Over the centuries the Goddess has provided protection not only from sickness but also from 'unholy incidents'.

Starting at dawn on the outskirts of the city, the Tamils set off for the temple, balancing on their heads brass jugs containing their offerings of sustenance - fresh milk - with which to annoint the Goddess, the Guardian of the Earth.

The role of female protecting deities, a counterbalance to the prevailing sexism of most faiths, is a key factor behind the popularity of this festival.

FESTIVAL:
Ascent of Croagh Padraig

Country, place and location:
Mountain of Croagh Patrick, near Westport, Co. Mayo, Rep. of Ireland

Religion:
Christian

Date of Celebration:
Garland Sunday - last Sunday in July

Even in pre-Christian times the mountain of Patrick was revered as a holy place and it was probably this attribute, as well as its remoteness, that drew Ireland's Patron Saint to it. Patrick spent the entire forty days of Lent in 441 AD on the summit of what was then known as *Cruachan Aigil*.

By the 11th century it had become a protected site and nowadays some 25,000 pilgrims make the ascent to the top of the 2,800ft high mountain on the last Sunday of July. Many start their ascent in the early hours of the morning and make the round trip of some ten miles entirely barefoot - as Patrick had done 1,500 years before. Despite the sharpness of the granite stones that surface the ascent route, most of them suffer neither cuts nor pain.

FESTIVAL:
Fiesta de la Virgen del Carmen

Country, Place and Location:
Paucartambo, Peru. The town lies at an altitude of 11,000 ft on the eastern slopes of the Andes, and is a gateway to the Amazon

Religion:
Pagan-Christian. Christianity in its hundreds of thousands of forms is the religion of one in three of the world's population

Date of Celebration:
July 15 -17

Nestling in a valley below Mount Ausangate (21,981ft) the remote town of Paucartambo celebrates annually, during the *Qechua* month of "earthly purification", the festival of *Mamacha Carmen*, or Earth Mother, the Patron Saint of the *Mestizo* population. For three days the town renews its faith, joy and hope for a better future. The festival dates from 1662 and the indigeneous population who participate in it fuse pre-Christian traditions with Christian mythology to enact a story of struggles and miracles. The festivities were originally organised by *mistis* (half-castes) who during the seventeenth century represented the higher class inhabitants of Paucartambo and they in turn were superseded by the *indigenista* (aboriginal or pure Indian) and later the Hispanics.

The holy image of the Virgin is, essentially, protected now by rival groups of dancers wearing costumes that reflect the turbulent history of the region. This is a *Danzaq o Tusuq*. The *Danzaq* is a mythical character representing the humanised form of an aggressive male goat that seduced young girls, conquered married women, consoled widows and terrorised teenagers.

FESTIVAL:
Fiesta de la Virgen del Carmen

Country, place and location:
Paucartambo, Peru. The town lies at an altitude of 11,000 ft on the eastern slopes of the Andes, and is a gateway to the Amazon

Religion:
Pagan-Christian. Christianity in its hundreds of thousands of forms is the religion of one in three of the world's population

Date of Celebration:
July 15 -17

1: Protectors of the image of the Virgin, these are two "Captains" of the *Qhapak Chunchu*

2: Two "Captains" of the *Qhapak Qolla* who consider themselves to be the true protectors of the Virgin. They are always accompanied by a Llama.

JUNE HIGHLIGHTS:

Belgium: Shrimp Festival, Oostduinkirke

Bolivia: Festividad de Nuestro Senor Jesus del Gran Poder, La Paz; Llama sacrifice, Potosi

China: Dragon Boat Festival; Corban; Kazak Wedding Festival; The Solemn Yet Joyous Festival of First-Breaking (Islamic)

Colombia: Festival Del Porro, San Pelayo, Cordoba

Cyprus: Kataklysmos, Festival of the Flood

England: Appleby Horse Fair, Cumbria; Summer Solstice, Stonehenge, Wilts

Hungary: Whitsuntide, Pecs

India: Id-ul-Zuha/Bakr-Id Muslim Festival

Indonesia: Sekaten Muslim Festival, North Square, Yogyakarta

Japan: Chagu-chagu Umakka Horse Festival, Morioka

Malta: Feast of St. Peter and St. Paul, Buskett, nr. Mdina

Morocco: Marrakech Folklore Festival, El Baddi Palace

Peru: Corpus Christi, Cuzco; Inti Raymi, Cuzco

Philippines: St. John the Baptist Feast Day, Balayan

Portugal: Cavalhadas de Vil de Moinhos, Viseu: Festas dos Santos Populares, Lisbon

Spain: Festival of San Juan, Soria; Pilgrimage to El Rocio, nr. Huelva, Almonte

St Vincent and Grenadines: Carnival

Thailand: Phi Ta Khon Festival, Amphoe Dan Sai, Loei

Tunisia: Ulysses Festival

Turkey: Feast of Sacrifice

U.S.A: Red Earth Festival, Oklahoma

Vietnam: Summer Solstice Day

JULY HIGHLIGHTS:
Australia: Boulia Desert Sands Camel Festival
Barbados: Crop Over Festival
Bolivia: Fiesta de Santiago, Torotoro
Czech Republic: Gypsy Festival, Brno
East Slovakia: Marian Pilgrimage to Levoca, nr. Spis
Finland: Pradznik Festival, Ilomantsi; Karelian Folklore Festival
India: Rath Yatra Temple Festival (Jagganath), Puri, Orissa; Pilgrimage to Amarnath Lingam Cave, Kashmir
Inner Mongolia Autonomous Region: Nadam Festival
Japan: Gion Matsuri, Kyoto
Korea: Boryeong Mud Festival, Boryeong
Laos: Khao Watsa "Rains Retreat" festival
Peru: Yawar Fiesta, Cotabambas (Apurimac) - the struggle between the Condor and the Bull
Spain: Fiesta de San Firmin, Pamplona
Tibet:: Paying Homage to the Holy Mountain Festival

AUGUST HIGHLIGHTS:
Bavaria: Alphornfest, Nesselwang
Belgium: Assumption Day, Bruges
Burma: Annual Nat Spirits Festival, Taungbyone, 20km north of Mandalay
Greece: Feast of St. Dennis, Island of Xanthi; Ascension of the Virgin, Island of Tinos
Haiti: Feast of the Assumption
Hungary: National Folklore Days, Tamasi
Ireland: Puck Fair, Killorglin
Italy: Joust of the Quintana, Asoli Piceno
Namibia: Maherero Day, Okahandja
Papua New Guinea: Mount Hagen Indigenous Cultural Festival
Peru: Canete week, Lima
Poland: Transfiguration, Grabarka, nr. border with Belarus
Portugal: Romaria do San Bento da Porta Aberta, nr. Geres
Singapore: Festival of the Hungy Ghosts
Sri Lanka: Esala Perahera, Kandy

SEPTEMBER HIGHLIGHTS:

Bolivia: Procession of San Roque, Tarija
Cambodia: Prachum Ben
England: Harvest Festival
Ethiopia: Ethiopian New Year's Day
India: Ganesh-Chaturthi Festival, Western Provinces
Israel: Rosh Hashanah
Italy: Lampedusa Island Festival; Historic Regatta, Venice; Palio, Florence
Laos: Festival of the Dead, Luang Prabang
Malta: Water Carnival of Our Lady of Victories
Mexico: Senora del Patricinio, Zacatecas
Morocco: Horse Festival, Tissa
Singapore: Moon-Cake Festival
Spain: Vendemia Festival, Jerez de la Frontera
Switzerland: Vintage Festival, Neuchatel
Tunisia: Cavalry Festival, Kairouan
Vietnam: Wandering Souls Day

OCTOBER HIGHLIGHTS:

Burma: Festival of Light, Taunggyi, Shan States
China: An Outing to Eight-Scene Park on Double-Nine Day, Western Hills, Beijing
Indonesia: Labuhan Alit Palace Ceremony, Top of Merapi and Lawu Mountains, nr Yogyakarta
India: Durga Puja/Dusserah
Israel: Sukkot Harvest Festival
Japan: Come Back Salmon Night, Abashiri, Eastern Hokkaido; Festival of the Ages of Heian Shrine, Kyoto
Malaysia: Festival for the Nine Emperor Gods
Peru: Lord of the Miracles, Lima
Portugal: Pilgrimage to Fatima Shrine, Vila Nova de Ourem
Seychelles: Kreol Festival
Singapore: Thimithi Fire Walking Festival
Spain: Saffron Rose Festival, Consuegra, Toledo
Thailand: Ascent of Tak Baht Dhevo, Uthai Thani

FESTIVAL:
Boi Ceremony

Country, Place and Location:
Zoroastrian Temple of Europe, Harrow, Middlesex, England

Religion:
Zoroastrianism. Began 2,600 years ago in Persia. Now about 125,000 adherents worldwide

Date of Celebration:
Continuously

The Cauldron of Fire is the symbol of Zoroastrianism. Fire burns away all evil and it can never be impure. Fire represents God and the maintenance of a sacred fire in Fire Temples - without allowing it to be extinguished - is an important feature. It is treated like a King and the Priests must feed it five times a day at prescribed hours. The crossed swords on the wall are a symbol of safeguarding the fire, whilst offerings of sandalwood are considered particularly meritorious for donors.

FESTIVAL:
Initiation to the Monkhood

Country, place and location:
Wat Po, Bangkok, Thailand

Religion:
Buddhist. founded 2500 years ago in India. There are over 300 million adherents worldwide

Date of Celebration:
Monthly

The primary goal of Buddhism is *Nirvana*, defined as the end of change, and literally meaning "to blow out" like a candle. The monastic life is necessary to attain *Nirvana* so children are encouraged to enter the monkhood, often for as little as two weeks 'to win merit'.

At an initiation ceremony in Wat Po, one of Thailand's most important temples, this teenager will change into saffron robes, denoting his new status as a novice monk.

FESTIVAL:
Pogrzebu i Triumfu Matki Bosej - Poland's Calvaries

Country, Place and Location:
Kalwaria Paclawska, near Ukrainian border, Poland

Religion:
Catholic

Date of Celebration:
August

Pilgrimages are an integral part of Polish religious life. It is estimated that about eight million people annually make pilgrimages to over four hundred shrines around the country dedicated to the Virgin Mary.

During the Funeral and Assumption of the Mother of God, this teenage pilgrim wears a Crown of Thorns. It is a day of indulgence when all those who participate in the ceremonies believe they can obtain total remission of their sins.

FESTIVAL:
Janmashtami

Country, Place and Location:
Bhaktivendanta Manor, Letchmore Heath, near Watford, England

Religion:
Hindu/International Society for Krishna Consciousness. In the last one hundred years more new religions have arrived in Europe than in the whole of recorded history before

Date of Celebration:
August, falling on the eighth day after the full moon

Janmashtami celebrates the annual birthday and re-appearance of Lord Krishna whom many consider to be God, or more precisely, the supreme personality of Godhead. He appeared 5000 years ago at Mathura, south of present day Delhi.

Many dances and devotional songs take place during the festive period. With the spread of ethnic Hindus across the world, Janmashtami is celebrated in many countries by a variety of people. These English-born *Mudralaya* dancers were celebrating in Watford.

FESTIVAL:
The Abbots Bromley Horn Dance

Country, Place and Location:
Abbots Bromley, Staffordshire, England

Religion:
Pagan Christian

Date of Celebration:
The date is determined by a quirky formula: the Monday following the first Sunday after the fourth of September

The Horn Dance - an ancient fertility celebration - is believed to be part of a pagan hunting ritual with origins that can be traced back to Saxon times; probably first performed at the Berthelmy Fair near Burton-on-Trent in 1226. The dancers carry around the lanes of rural Staffordshire six pairs of enormous Reindeer horns, of great antiquity, which have been carbon dated to 1065 - around the time of the Norman Conquest. There are references in the Bible to the wearing of deer horns as a sign of strength.

FESTIVAL:
Fete de Saint-Michel

Country, Place and Location:
Mont-Saint-Michel, Normandy, France. The pilgrimage starts from the village of Genets on the north shore of the *baie*

Religion:
Catholic

Date of Celebration:
September

Pilgrimage is the oldest form of package holiday; indeed the word holiday comes from 'holy day'. In the Christian tradition a high place such as Mont St. Michel is dedicated to the fighting Archangel St. Michael who combats evil and protects the devout pilgrim through life.

Mont St. Michel, *le merveile de l'occident*, the Wonder of the West, was dedicated to St. Michael in AD 708 by Aubert, Bishop of Avranches, following a series of dreams in which the Archangel ordered him to transform the rock into a place of worship. From then on the island became one of the most important places of pilgrimage in the western world, alongside Rome, Jerusalem and Santiago de Compostela.

For centuries the waters in the bay surrounding the Mount have been the centre of one of the strongest tides in the world. On rare occasions during the year the tide recedes ten miles out into the bay.

At the time of this low tide, hundreds of pilgrims walk across the bay, as they have done on major feast days for at least six hundred years, to venerate St. Michael - Guardian of the Gates to Paradise.

FESTIVAL:
Nuestra Senora Del Pilar

Country, Place and Location:
Zaragoza, Arragon, Spain

Religion:
Catholic

Date of Celebration:
September

According to local legend the Virgin Mary, whilst still living in Jerusalem, miraculously came to Zaragoza to visit St. James the Apostle who, at that time, was living on the banks of the River Ebro in Spain, teaching the Gospel to his early converts. Her visit is said to have taken place on a quite specific date, January 2 40 AD.

From this time, a massive festival has grown which now attracts upwards of 500,000 pilgrims who bring the City to a complete standstill during the week of celebrations as they honour the Virgin.

Dancers and Guitarists perform outside the Basilica de Nuestra Senora Del Pilar, and the over-riding sound is that of the dancer's castanets.

FESTIVAL:
Vegetarian Festival

Country, place and location:
Phuket Town, Phuket, Thailand

Religion:
Chinese Traditional

Date of Celebration:
October

The devotees who inflict these seemingly horrendous acts of mutilation on themselves are merely participating in the Chinese *Song Dao* ceremony - in honour of the nine Emperor Gods who control people's destinies - the rituals of which stretch back 160 years.

These acts of apparent torture are performed in the belief that they will achieve great merit for the sufferers, bring them a trouble-free year while at the same time freeing them of any future spiritual problems.

What is extraordinary is that, however fearsome the implements used for impaling, there is no blood and certainly this young man appears to be in little pain.

FESTIVAL:
Phaung Daw U

Country, Place and Location:
Lake Inle, Burma (Myanmar)

Religion:
Buddhist. Founded 2500 years ago in India. There are over 300 million adherents worldwide

Date of Celebration:
18 days during the period of the full moon of *thadingyut*, which usually falls between September and November

Inle Lake is the home of the indigenous *Intha* (the 'sons of the lake') who are believed to have migrated here from south-east Burma around 1393. Today, there are 80,000 of them who live on sixty-four floating villages scattered across the lake. The objects of the *Intha* people's veneration are five short stumpy statues from the 12th century which reside in the Phaung Daw U *paya*, one of the three most sacred shrines in Burma. This annual festival provides an opportunity for all the 'sons of the lake' to pay homage to four of these images which are transported daily to a different *kyaung* (lake monastery) by an enormous golden *karaweik* (barge) - an ancient Burmese ceremonial vessel carved in the shape of a swan.

1: The aquatic procession of the *Karaweik* is preceeded by an escort of long *hley* (canoes) crewed by one hundred oarsmen. This one is being rowed through one of the many lagoons within the lake.

2: Tall grasses waving gently in the wind appear to mimic the grace and fluidity of the *Kachathe* dancers who form an important element of the huge daily aquatic procession.

NOVEMBER HIGHLIGHTS:

Austria: St Leopold's Festival, Klosterneuberg
Bolivia: Day of of the Dead
Ecuador: Day of the Dead
Holland: St. Nicholas, Amsterdam
India: Divali
Mexico: Day of the Dead
Philippines: Horse-Fight Festival, Lem-Lunay, Lake Sebu, Mindanao
Tibet: Fairy Maiden Festival

DECEMBER HIGHLIGHTS:

Bahamas: Junkanoo
Bulgaria: Koledouvane
Colombia: Fiesta de la Cana de Azucar, Cali
Guatemala: Festival of St. Thomas, Chichicastenango
Israel: Hanukah
Madeira: Festival of St. Sylvester
Mexico: Fiesta de Guadalupe, Noragachi, Sierra Tarahumara
Philippines: Grand Lantern Festival, San Fernando (Pampanga), Luzon
Slovenia: Day of the Innocent Children
Sweden: Festival of St. Lucia
Switzerland: Klauslagen, Kussnacht; Escalade Festival, Geneva
Tunisia: Tozeur Desert Festival

Across the globe there are thousands of annual celebrations, and the events highlighted here are only a mere indication. Some I have mentioned are culturally well-known, others extremely unusual and esoteric. Many of the dates for these celebrations are fixed by the Gregorian Calendar (365 days) - and never change. Others may change due to climatic conditions such as drought, or be postponed or cancelled because it is deemed that the timimg is not auspicious. Islamic festivals are determined by the Muslim Calendar, which is Lunar, and the dates therefore change every year. References to the majority of events in this Calendar can be found through appropriate Internet Search Engines. Determining the dates for festivals can be complicated so check, and re-check, the dates before embarking!

FESTIVAL:
Galungan-Kuningan

Country, Place and Location:
Bali, Indonesia

Religion:
A blend of Hindu, Buddhist, Javanese and ancient indigenous beliefs

Date of Celebration:
November

The Balinese worship Brahma, Ganesh, Shiva and Vishnu and believe strongly in magic and the power of spirits. They have celebrations for every facet of life - including births, weddings, teeth-pulling, rice-planting and rain-stopping. To determine these dates, not only do they use the traditional lunar calendar but they also utilize their own *wuku* calendar of 210 days, effectively celebrating the New Year every seven months.

The great New Year holiday of Galungan-Kuningan celebrates the victory of Virtue *Dharma* over Evil *Adharma* and lasts for ten days. During this time the ancestral spirits come down to Earth to live in the homes of their descendants.

The *wahi* is danced for these spirits, not for an audience, and I was extremely fortunate to see these dancers, wreathed in clouds of incense, performing in the inner courtyard of their village temple.

FESTIVAL:
Kartika Purnima

Country, Place and Location:
Pushkar, Rajasthan, India

Religion:
Hindu. One of the world's oldest living religions which predates recorded history. Over 800 million adherents worldwide

Date of Celebration:
The five days preceeding the full moon in November

Pushkar has been a pilgrimage destination since the 4th century AD.

Bathing at any of the *tirthas* - India's holiest places - washes away sins, but only the lake at Pushkar, the most sacred in all India, "makes a sinner free from all the deadliest sins; to die at this place is salvation giving". For, according to the *Sadhus*, the Lord Brahma declared that "during these five days, all the gods will remain present at Pushkar and bless the people".

I came upon this vista of the lakeside in the early morning of the first day of the festivities.

FESTIVAL:
Pushkar Camel Fair

Country, place and location:
Pushkar, Rajasthan, India

Religion:
Hindu. One of the world's oldest living religions which predates recorded history. Over 800 million adherents worldwide

Date of Celebration:
The five days preceeding the full moon in November

Even though Pushkar is one of India's most holy places, the Camel Fair that is held concurrently with the sacred ceremonies is the largest in all of India. This group were on their way to the Camel Fair to participate in the gigantic *mela* (fair) set up to entertain the hundreds of thousands of devotees who attend the bathing ceremonies of *Kartika Purnima* (QV).

FESTIVAL:
The Sema, or Mevlevi, Ceremony

Country, Place and Location:
Konya, Turkey

Religion:
Islam. Founded by the Prophet Mohammed about 1,400 years ago in Arabia. Islam is the world's fastest growing religion; there are about 950 million adherents worlwide

Celaleddin Rumi, the Mevlana, was born in 1207 and was one of the great mystics of Islam and founder of the 'Whirling' Mevlevi Dervishes

Date of Celebration:
December 10 -17

The 'Whirling' Ceremony, or *Sema*, is a means of freeing the Dervish from earthly bondage and abandonment to God's love. Its ultimate purpose is to effect a union with God. The clothes worn have a symbolic significance: the camel-hair hat represents a tombstone and the white skirt a funerary shroud.

FESTIVAL:
Festival du Sahara

Country, Place and Location:
Doux, Tunisia

Religion:
Islam. Founded by the Prophet Mohammed about 1,400 years ago in Arabia. Islam is the world's fastest growing religion; there are about 950 million adherents worlwide

Date of Celebration:
End of December

Formerly known as *La Fete des Dromedaires*, this is the oldest and most famous Tunisian festival. It provides a secular opportunity for the tribal Berber of the northern Sahara to celebrate the end of one year and the beginning of the next. It represents today the liberal face of Islam.

FURTHER READING

GENERAL:
Dates and Meanings of Religious and Other Festivals: Dr. John Walshe
W. Foulsham and Co. London 1989
Dictionary of Festivals: J. C.Cooper *Thorsons, London 1995*
Faiths and Festivals: Martin Palmer *Ward Lock, London 1984*
Festivals and Celebrations: Rowland Purton *Basil Blackwell, Oxford 1989*
Festivals in World Religions: edited by Adam Brown *Shap 1986*
Festivals in World Religions: Peter Woodward *Shap Working Party, 1998*
Ritual: Magnum *Andre Deutsch London 1990*
The Spiritual Tourist: Mick Brown *Bloomsbury, London 1999*

SPECIFIC:
Burma: Caroline Courtauld *Odyssey Publications, Hong Kong, 1999*
Burma As It Was, As It Is and As It Will Be: Sir George Scott *George Redway, 1886*
Espana Oculta: Cristina Garcia Rodero *Lunwerg Editores, Madrid, 1989*
Festivals of India: *National Book Trust, India 1982*
Guatemalan Guide: Peter Glassman *Passport Press, New York 1987*
Hindu Feasts, Fasts and Ceremonies: *Srishti Publishers, New Delhi 1999*
Hindu Gods and Goddesses: Ashish Khokar *Rupa and Co. New Delhi 1993*
Island of Bali: Miguel Covarrubias *Periplus, Jakarta, Indonesia 1973*
Les-Saintes-Maries-de-la-Mer: Alain Albaric *Editions Vent Large, Paris 1998*
Misteria: Adam Bujak *Wydawnictwo Warsaw, 1989*
Sadhus - Holy Men of India: Dolf Hartsuiker *Thames and Hudson, London 1993*
Thai Festivals: W. Warren and L. Invernizzi Tettoni *Asia Books, Bangkok, 1989*
The Living Legend of St. Patrick: Alannah Hopkin *Grafton Books, London 1989*
Touching Tibet: Niema Ash *Travellers Eye, Bridgnorth, Shropshire UK 1999*